This book belongs to:

______________________________

Made in the USA
Las Vegas, NV
27 November 2023

81556759R00066